Akachi Adimora-Ezeigbo

The Prize

Illustrated by
Shirley Tourret

Series Editor: Rod Nesbitt

Heinemann Educational Publishers
A division of Heinemann Publishers (Oxford) Ltd
Halley Court, Jordan Hill, Oxford OX2 8EJ

Heinemann Educational Books (Nigeria) Ltd
PMB 5205, Ibadan
Heinemann Educational Boleswa
PO Box 10103, Village Post Office, Gaborone, Botswana

FLORENCE PRAGUE PARIS MADRID
ATHENS MELBOURNE JOHANNESBURG
AUCKLAND SINGAPORE TOKYO
CHICAGO SAO PAULO

© Akachi Adimora-Ezeigbo 1994

First published by Heinemann Educational Publishers in 1994

The right of Akachi Adimora-Ezeigbo to be identified as the author of this work has been asserted by her in accordance with the Copyright, Designs and Patents Act 1988

British Library Cataloguing in Publication Data
A catalogue record for this book is available
from the British Library

ISBN 0 435 89173 1

Glossary
Difficult words are listed alphabetically on page 29

Printed and bound in Great Britain by
George Over Limited, Rugby and London

94 95 96 97 98 10 9 8 7 6 5 4 3 2 1

Onyema sat on a mat in front of her house. She was opening melon seeds for the evening meal. Her twin brother, Ogbonnaya, was in the village. He had gone to play football with his friends.

Onyema looked up and saw her teacher walking towards her.

'Good evening, sir,' she said.

'Good evening, Onyema,' replied Mr Nwiboko. 'Is your father at home?'

'Yes, sir. He's in the house.'

Mr Nwiboko knocked on the door.

'Teacher, please come in,' Onyema's father said. 'How are you and your family?'

He was a farmer and had just returned from the farm. He offered Mr Nwiboko a chair.

'Thank you,' said Mr Nwiboko. He sat down, and coughed to clear his throat.

'Mr Agu,' he began, 'I came to find out why your daughter hasn't filled in the scholarship forms. She can do very well in the examination.'

Mr Agu looked angry.

'It's my wish that only my son, Ogbonnaya, should fill in the forms,' he said.

'But Onyema is very clever,' the teacher replied. 'In fact she's the best pupil in mathematics in the class.'

'I don't believe in educating girls beyond primary school,' Mr Agu said. 'It's just a waste of time and money.'

'But–' began Mr Nwiboko.

'I have nothing more to say,' Onyema's father said firmly.

Mr Nwiboko left the house. Onyema was very sad as she watched him go. She had listened to everything her father and the teacher had said. She wanted so much to go to secondary school. She began to cry.

'Why is Papa so cruel to me?' she sobbed. 'I'm only thirteen. Why does he want to marry me off to Onyia? He's old and fat and ugly!'

Later, Onyema told her mother about her teacher's visit. Mrs Agu promised to try to help.

'Oh, thank you, Mama!' exclaimed Onyema, not knowing exactly what her mother would do. 'The forms cost ten naira,' Onyema added.

'All right, my child,' said Mrs Agu. 'You know I want you to take the scholarship exam with your brother.'

Mrs Agu sold palm oil in the market. She had five children, but Onyema was her favourite.

A few days later, Mrs Agu came to Ezzikwo Community School to see Mr Nwiboko. She had come to pay for Onyema's scholarship forms.

The pupils were out, working in the garden. Onyema saw her mother and ran to meet her.

'Where's your brother?' Mrs Agu asked with a smile.

'He's gone with some of the other boys to cut sticks.'

'Go back to work now,' Mrs Agu said. 'I'm going to speak to Mr Nwiboko.'

Onyema's school was one of the schools in the Ezzikwo Local Government Area. Every year each school sent its cleverest pupils to sit for the scholarship examination.

Mr Eke, the headmaster, spoke to all the final year pupils.

'The government is giving three scholarships this year,' he said. 'We want pupils from Ezzikwo Community School to win all three scholarships. I want everyone to work their hardest.'

Mr Nwiboko worked very hard with the pupils in Form Six. This was the senior class. Boys and girls in this class would sit the scholarship examination.

He even organised extra lessons after school. All the boys stayed for the extra lessons, but only a few of the girls could stay. Most of them went home to help their mothers working in the house or selling things in the market.

Sometimes Onyema was able to stay for extra lessons. Her mother would come home early to do the work in the house. Her father didn't know about this. He would be angry if he found out.

Mr Agu often told Onyema to do things for him after school. But Ogbonnaya was free to stay for extra lessons.

It was always Onyema who fetched water, and gathered firewood and cooked the evening meals.

One Saturday evening, Onyema was sitting beside her mother. Mrs Agu was stitching her husband's shirt.

The younger children, two boys and a little girl, were playing on the floor.

'Mama, I'm tired of my life,' Onyema said suddenly.

'Don't say that!' Mrs Agu said. 'Your life is just beginning.'

'But, Mama, I don't want to marry Onyia,' cried Onyema. 'I'll run away if Papa tries to make me marry.'

Mrs Agu was very sad.

Mrs Agu remembered the day she married Onyema's father. She too had been about thirteen. Then four years later, she had had the twins. She was grateful that she was able to keep them. Her grandmother had told her that twins were killed at birth. It had been the custom for many years. The custom changed after the white people arrived.

She turned to Onyema.

'Don't worry,' she said. 'Something good will happen.'

Onyema felt better. She knew her mother was on her side. And Mr Nwiboko helped with her mathematics and English. They both wanted her to win a scholarship.

Onyema studied very hard whenever she could. She didn't want to disappoint them. On the way to fetch water or firewood, she went over the day's lessons in her mind. Mr Nwiboko had told her that this was a good way to study.

It was a month before the scholarship examination. Onyema and some of the other pupils were standing outside their classroom.

The boys talked cheerfully about their future careers. The girls just stood and listened.

'I'm going to be a doctor,' Ogbonnaya said proudly.

'I want to be a pilot,' said Ofodum.

'No, I'm going to be an accountant,' shouted Ibe eagerly.

'I want to be a journalist,' said James.

'Who wants to be a teacher?' said Ezeobu.

'Teachers are poor!' shouted Ogbonnaya.

Everybody laughed.

Then Onyema spoke.

'I'm going to be an engineer,' she said.

Some of the boys laughed rudely.

'An engineer!' mocked Nwokolo. He was Onyia's youngest brother, but the oldest pupil in Form Six. 'Girls can't be engineers.'

'Yes, they can,' Onyema insisted.

'Remember, you're my brother's wife,' Nwokolo said.

'Leave her alone!' Ogbonnaya said.

Ogbonnaya did not like his father's plan.

One day, Onyema was washing clothes in Lake Nwokpuru. Her friend, Njide, was with her.

'Hey, engineer!' a voice shouted.

Onyema looked up and saw Nwokolo. He was carrying a fishing hook and line and some worms in a cup.

Onyema said nothing. She just went on with her work.

Nwokolo was annoyed by her silence.

'Have you lost your tongue?' he said angrily. 'Can't you speak to your brother-in-law?'

'Silence is the best way to answer a fool,' Onyema replied.

'Just remember. In March next year, you'll become my brother's wife,' Nwokolo shouted in a rage.

Marriage ceremonies in their village usually took place in March.

'Then you'll be the engineer in my brother's kitchen,' he added with a laugh.

'Listen, Nwokolo,' cried Onyema. 'Your brother is wasting his time. I'll never be his wife. I'm going to be a real engineer.'

When Onyema arrived home, her parents were sitting in front of the house, talking. Ogbonnaya was standing by the door. He and his father had just come back from the farm.

Ogbonnaya helped Onyema to spread the clothes on the line. He thanked her for washing his clothes. He gave her some of the wild fruit he had brought from the farm. He tried to talk but Onyema was very quiet.

After supper, Mr Agu fell asleep in an armchair. Mrs Agu was counting the money from the day's sale of palm oil. The younger children had gone to bed.

Ogbonnaya was looking at his English textbook, trying to study in the dim light.

Onyema sat in the corner, thinking of her talk with Nwokolo at the lake. She didn't know what to do.

Her thoughts made her very unhappy. She couldn't understand why her father wanted her to marry so early. He had told her Onyia was a rich cloth merchant in Kano.

Onyema didn't care if he was the richest man in the world. She wanted to go to secondary school.

'Papa,' she burst out, suddenly. 'I've told you, I won't be Onyia's wife! I'm going to be an engineer.'

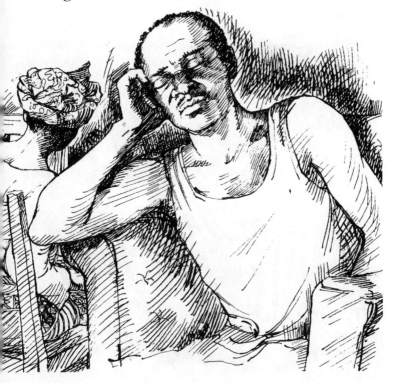

Mr Agu woke with a jump.

'What did you say?' Mr Agu asked sleepily.

Onyema was not afraid. She always spoke up whenever she had anything to say.

'I said I won't marry Onyia. I want to go to secondary school.'

'Papa, please, don't make her marry Onyia,' Ogbonnaya said miserably.

'Shut up, both of you!' shouted Mr Agu. 'She's going to marry Onyia and that's my last word.'

Onyema decided to study even harder. She was even more determined now to win a scholarship.

'If I get the scholarship, maybe Papa will change his mind about the marriage,' Onyema thought. 'Maybe I'll get to secondary school.'

With her mother's help, she stayed in school more often for extra lessons. Sometimes she studied in the house or under the mango tree near the house.

One day, a week before the examination, Onyema arrived home late from school. She had stayed to assist some of her friends with their mathematics.

'Why are you so late?' Mr Agu asked angrily.

Mrs Agu rushed out of the kitchen.

'It's my fault. I sent her to my sister's house to deliver a message,' she explained.

She quickly took Onyema into the house. She didn't want her daughter upset before the examination.

At last the day of the scholarship examination arrived. It was a Saturday in November. About three hundred pupils from fifteen schools had filled in the forms for the scholarship. The twins did not have far to travel, because the examination was held in the Town Hall in Ezzikwo.

Onyema and Ogbonnaya were very nervous, but they were determined to do their best. Nwokolo and the other pupils from Ezzikwo Community School looked nervous too as they went into the hall.

When the examination results arrived, Mr Eke called an assembly to announce them.

Mr Nwiboko did not go to the assembly. He went to speak to Mr and Mrs Agu.

'Your child has won a scholarship,' he told them.

'Aha,' Mr Agu said happily, 'Ogbonnaya's going to be a doctor.'

'Which child?' Mrs Agu asked quietly.

'Onyema,' Mr Nwiboko said. 'She's the only pupil from our school.'

Mr Agu looked surprised.

That afternoon Onyema and Ogbonnaya walked home from school together.

'I wish we had both won a scholarship,' said Onyema.

'I'm glad you won,' Ogbonnaya said. 'You deserve it. The scholarship is the prize for your cleverness and hard work.'

They walked on in silence.

Then Ogbonnaya added, 'Papa will pay my fees to secondary school, anyway. Remember, he wants me to be a doctor.'

They laughed happily.

The twins walked up to the house. Mr Agu came out, followed by Mrs Agu and the younger children.

'Well done, my daughter,' he said, holding out his hand.

'Thank you, Papa,' replied Onyema. 'So you've heard?' She looked at her mother.

'Yes, Mr Nwiboko told us,' Mrs Agu said.

Mr Agu reached out and drew the twins close.

'Well,' he said, 'Onyia will just have to find himself another wife. My daughter is too clever for him.'

'Why did Papa change his mind?' Onyema asked her mother that evening.

Mrs Agu smiled.

'At first he was angry,' she said. 'He wanted Ogbonnaya to win a scholarship. Then he smiled and said that his daughter really was clever.'

'What did he do?'

'He started to laugh. He said you could go to school and marry later – if you were not too clever for the men in the village.'

Questions

1 Write down three customs which the author describes in the story. Are these good customs or bad customs?
2 Why does Mr Nwiboko come to visit Onyema's father the first time?
3 Why does Mr Agu refuse to do what Mr Nwiboko asks?
4 Why does Onyema not want to marry Onyia?
5 What does Onyema decide to do if her father makes her marry Onyia?
6 Why does Nwokolo say that girls can't be engineers?
7 Ogbonnaya wants to be a doctor, but he is not worried when Onyema wins the scholarship. Why?
8 What makes Mr Agu change his mind about Onyema winning the scholarship?

Activities

1 Make a list of the customs and traditions of the people in your town or village. Then with a partner or a group make a list of the customs and traditions of people in other parts of the world.
2 In a group discuss each of the customs or traditions you listed and decide which are good and which are bad.

3 Draw a picture of Onyema fetching water for her mother.

4 Imagine you won a prize – not a scholarship, but a lot of money. Write a short description telling what you would do with the money. What would you buy? Where would you go? What presents would you buy?

Glossary

accountant (page 13) someone who looks after the accounts and money in a business

custom (page 11) something that people always did in the past, or still do now

determined (page 21) deciding to do something no matter what happens

disappoint (page 12) not do something people hoped you would do

engineer (page 14) someone who works with machines or electricity, or who builds roads or bridges

grateful (page 11) give thanks for something

journalist (page 13) someone who writes for a newspaper or magazine

organised (page 8) planned and then did something

scholarship (page 2) free education won by doing well in an examination

The Junior African Writers Series is designed to provide interesting and varied African stories both for pleasure and for study. There are five graded levels in the series. Three new levels of JAWS are currently being developed for younger readers. These full-colour JAWS Starter levels will be available in 1995.

Level 2 is suited to readers who have been studying English for four to five years. The content and language have been carefully controlled to increase fluency in reading.

Content The plots are simple and the number of characters is kept to a minimum. The information is presented in small manageable amounts and the illustrations reinforce the text.

Language Reading is a learning experience and, although the choice of words is carefully controlled, new words, important to the story, are also introduced. These are contextualised, recycled through the story and explained in the glossary. They also appear in other stories at Level 2.

Glossary Difficult words which learners may not know and which are not made clear in the illustrations have been listed alphabetically at the back of the book. The definitions refer to the way the word is used in the story and the page reference is for the word's first use.

Questions and **Activities** The questions give useful comprehension practice and ensure that the reader has followed and understood the story. The activities develop themes and ideas introduced and can be done as pairwork or groupwork in class, or as homework.

Other JAWS titles at Level 2

Mr Kalogo's Factory, Paulinos Vincent Magombe, 0 435 89175 8

The Strange Piece of Paper, Patricia Sealey, 0 435 89174 X

Bottletop Michael, Robert Dickson, 0 435 89170 7

The Buried Treasure, Akachi Adimora-Ezeigbo, 0 435 89169 3

The Angel Who Wore Shoes, Dan Fulani, 0 435 89172 3

The Ghost of Ratemo, James Ngumy, 0 435 89171 5